Don't Let Stress Keep You From Success!

Dr. Rosie Ramos

a  publication

Don't Let Stress Keep You From Success!

a DSTL Arts publication

The work in this book was written by Dr. Rosie Ramos, a participant in DSTL Arts's Poet/Artist Development Program, and first printed in April, 2024 by DSTL Arts publishing in Los Angeles, CA, U.S.A. All rights reserved. No part of this book may be reproduced in any form without written permission from the publisher.

Cover and Book Design: Luis Antonio Pichardo

Additional Illustrations: Melissa Zuniga and Walter Steve Zuniga

ISBN: 978-1-946081-73-5

10 9 8 7 6 5 4 3 2 1

www.DSTLArts.org

Los Angeles, CA

Table of Contents

Don't Let Stress Keep You From Success

Prologue

Hello Readers,

Stress affects us all at various points in life, and recently, I found myself reflecting on how I deal with stress. I distinctly remember being a young person and not fully understanding how stress affected every aspect of my life, from my social connections to schooling, regarding my health, to family life.

This chapbook was written through genuine heartfelt testimonies shared by young people who, through their life experiences and stressors, hope to help others feel less alone.

Each young person who contributed to this chapbook used their own, unique voice to express how stress has affected their life. Each person had a choice to have their real name mentioned (per their story) or to create a pen name. Each selected their own pen name.

I spent the past 35 years as a community advocate and social worker for families, teens, and children. Throughout the years, I have witnessed incredible stories of hardship. Hardships often turn into beautiful stories of growth and success, and I am honored to translate these inspiring stories of young people into art and poetry. In doing so, I've strived to embody their essential message while highlighting underlying themes.

I introduced their stories in a haiku poem, then created a free verse poem to reflect their raw bluntness, passion, pain, and resilience.

At the end of this chapbook are resources for you or a friend (current as of this chapbook's original publishing date). I hope you know that there are many people, in many places, ready and eager to help you.

To all of the young people who inspired this chapbook, thank you so much for using your voices and sharing your stories and life challenges that have caused, or continue to cause you, stressors as you contend to assert yourself and succeed in finding a balance of calmness while counterattacking your stressors through life.

My time spent with each young person whose stories you will shortly read was invaluable. From the bottom of my heart, I am blessed and privileged to have met such wonderful and inspiring people who, through their stories, demonstrated compassion, advocacy, and responsibility for others.

Mil gracias and stay strong!

–*Dr. Rosie Ramos*

MY VOICE MATTERS

Haiku and Free Verse Poems inspired by Luz's story:

My feelings and thoughts
tossed in a savage vortex,
STOP! My VOICE MATTERS!

When parents express
"Hey, stop complaining so much!"
I do not feel heard.

Growing up, I often found myself on the streets instead of at home. It wasn't all bad, though. I was blessed to have good friends in my neighborhood where I could drop in without notice and hang out for hours. I thank God that my male friends did not rape me, and none of the men in my life (my friend's brothers, dads, uncles, abuelos, etc.) ever harmed me. I have heard stories of girls like me who have been raped and nothing much happened to punish their abusers. Thank God I was respected outside of home as I went through hard times with my mom.

My friends and I drank and liked to smoke but we

did not do heavy drugs. Most of my friends' parents valued my feelings; they believed and respected me because I was polite and respectful to them. They fed my heart with acceptance and my stomach with great Latino, homemade food when I was hungry.

I often needed a break from my mom, a single woman who worked hard to make ends meet, but who did not bother to care about what I had to say. My feelings meant nothing to her, and it was always just her and me. There was no one else at home to turn to for emotional support!

At seventeen, my friends and I were getting ready to graduate from high school. Prom, dances, and hanging out with our friends was all we wanted to do. We didn't want to worry about our home life crap because our focus was on finishing school, maybe going to college, or getting a full-time job to buy a car. I'm not stupid; I wanted to maintain good grades. It paid off because now, I am in college.

Living with a very demanding, bitchy, and selfish parent is very stressful. In my situation, I could never get a word in with my mom. She did not value my opinion, so when I refused to be her slave around the house, she negatively labeled me. I love her, but I hate her.

As a young person trying to make it in life, it's hard

and shitty to feel unsupported by my mom. I am twenty-one now, but even as a teen, I fought to be respected by my mom because I know that MY VOICE MATTERS!

MY VOICE MATTERS!

Seventeen-year-old, mature, and school smart
    ¡LIMPIA LA CASA!
My single mom—Sooo damn Bossy—I MUST STUDY!

Talking, yelling, ignoring her squawking voice
    ¡NO ME RESPETAS!
Respect goes both ways, MOM! Listen to me!

It always has to be about her!
    ¡LUZ, HÁZME CASO!
My MOM has empty feelings—no compassion.

I seek out FRIENDS to feel my lonely void
    ¡SIEMPRE EN CALLE!
So bitchy! No real daughter-mother love!

Must leave my hellhole "safe home"—I HATE IT!
    ¡MALA HIJA MIA!
My friend's mothers hug me—LISTEN!

I can't expect Mom to LOVE and LISTEN to me.
My mom's mother never showed her LOVE...
    "Mom, te quiero!"

Parental Deception is a Reality

Haiku and Free Verse Poems inspired by Felix the Cat's story:

> *I am not crazy!*
> *Parental deceit is real,*
> *Thought it was "normal."*

Call me "Felix the Cat" because I have nine lives. Believe me, I need them all. I am a single child, born to very judgmental and opinionated parents who always believed their word is gold.

As a child, I was punished for showing anger, throwing fits, and challenging my parents. That is what kids do; I was acting normal. My parents never showed me any compassion or parental love. They messed with my head at a very young age, saying that I was a "bad child" and that my opinion did not count. I was constantly sent to my room for hours for my "bad behavior," but most of the time, I did not know what I did wrong. As a teen, I got involved in drugs to escape the turmoil in my home. I started to feel anger and hatred towards my parents because they never took the time to hear me. They constantly put me down.

"You are never going to amount to anything."

"Cut your awful, long hair. You look feminine."

"You are a big disappointment, especially to your father."

It was a repetitive reminder that I do not count in this family!

I grew up feeling oppressed and emotionally trapped by my evil, selfish, narrow-minded, biological parents. Sadly, I thought that was normal. I am learning the difference through therapy and doing the difficult, emotional work to reprogram my thoughts from negative to positive. I am trying to build up my self-worth. Man, this rebuilding takes a long time, but I know I have to keep working on myself to undo the emotional damage caused by my parents, something they will never admit!

Unfortunately, I still live at home because I cannot afford to live on my own. I still get backlash as my parents constantly judge me. In front of my friends, they say things like, "You dress as if you're homeless with those torn-up jeans," and "Music and theatre will get you nowhere, but then we don't expect much from you."

They have opinions about everything: how I speak, my

hairstyle bothers them, what I wear, who my friends are, and what I study. They absolutely hate that my studies focus on music and theatre. Everything about me (in their eyes) is WRONG!

From birth, they must have prophesied that I would disappoint them.

I know it's silly and stupid, but I like saying I'm Felix the Cat because I have nine lives—I revive from my emotional pain and the danger I feel from them not supporting me. To me, that means I am a true survivor! At this point in my life, it's better to live happily and be okay with laughing and joking than drowning in depression, and anger, and drugs. I can't change my parents, but I certainly can and will change ME!!!

Parental Deception is a Reality

Two humans had sex and made a baby (ME)—and
    have shown that they don't care
They turn my words against me
My light of hope is nowhere in sight—I need to
    breathe fresh air.

I'm not crazy—so what the hell is happening to me?

My emotions keep slipping through my heart, body,
    and fingers
I have trouble holding onto my thoughts
Floating in the air like flimsy kites on skinny, brittle
    strings, they linger.

I'm not crazy—so what the hell is happening to me?

I live with dysfunctional and toxic parents
They overwhelm me, take pleasure in manipulating
    and gaslighting me
Causing me to doubt myself and feel anxious and
    angry—nothing between us but arguments!

I'm not crazy—so what the hell is happening to me?

I can't cope, so I hit the dope and still can't function

My home has dark walls, and the atmosphere smells
     like dead old rancid fish—that dysfunction,
and no windows for outsiders to see their abuse
     towards me!

I'm not crazy—so what the hell is happening to me?

I feel like I'm losing ME—how wrong they have
     influenced ME
God! Where are you in this dark, pitfall, and inhumane
     part of this house?
Hey, Felix the Cat!—so where are you?—"Here kitty,
     kitty!"

I'm not crazy—so what the hell is happening to me?

I have horrible nightmares of my two larger-than-life
     parents, the Godzillas tearing off my limbs
While insulting me with their high-pitched, ear-piercing
     screeching voices
My anxieties are heightened, so how do I regain my
     inner strength—God forgive their sins.

I'm not crazy—so what the hell is happening to me?

I don't feel like myself—never did because my brain
     is scattered
As a kid, as a teen, and now a young adult—how do
     I pick up the pieces?
I've been trying to get away from ME—I was wrongly
     guided to believe I don't matter!

I'm not crazy—so what the hell is happening to me?

Don't judge me—let me be opinionated, angry, a
jokester, without guilt—instead, to thrive!
YOU were supposed to love and support me as
compassionate, caring parents

But you didn't. YOU don't care—why should I care
about myself?
WAIT! You ARE NOT Crazy! Breathe... Felix the Cat,
because you've got nine lives!

I KNOW WHO I AM

Haiku and Free Verse Poems inspired by Sonia's story:

Child, Folx, Siblings, Friends...
Don't Judge!! I KNOW WHO I AM.
They, She, Theirs, Ze, Her...

I am 20 years old, and I identify as nonbinary. I will move out soon but still live at home because it's too expensive to get my own place. What is most important to me, regardless of my sexual orientation, is that I'm an individual and deserve to be respected, especially by my parents and family members. I admit that la cultura, religion, and family are my challenging obstacles and weaknesses; my overall stressors.

At 15 years old, I came out to my friends and they were happy for me. I considered myself a true friend because I was there for them in good and bad times. Some of my friends abandoned me when I felt most alone and needed a safe place when my family rejected me for being gay.

I told my parents that I wanted them to accept me for who I am. I am the rebel child in my family. I did well in school, so my parents overlooked my rebelliousness except when I told them I liked girls. I wanted the freedom to bring girls home, go out with girls, and later have a girlfriend, but my parents freaked out on me. I wasn't even thinking about sex—I am sure they were!

My mom sounded so prejudiced when she told me that no daughter of hers was going to "bring disgrace to the family." My siblings, especially my brother, would constantly tell me that my thoughts and feelings were "not normal," so they would try  to "fix me" so that my mom would accept me again. My mom would have my brother escort me to school dances (like a damn date), even if I didn't want to go.

My father is an alcoholic, yet the family accepts him because he is the breadwinner and mainly drinks at home. My mother accepts her drunk husband, but not me. How crazy is my mom to be okay with an alcoholic husband but reject her teen daughter?

When they first found out that I was gay, they used our traditional cultural norms to shame me. My mom claims I've caused many embarrassments among the family and community friends. She told me that I was going to hell for my sins. My parents overreacted and were punitive because they are prejudiced against Lesbians or gay folx. Sadly, I can't change how they think.

I went through stress, sadness, and depression for about four years trying to convince my parents that I was still me, their daughter. I've been wishing for them to stop judging me because I know who I am. To love me for me, for being a good person, is all I ask. When I was about eighteen, I wanted to commit suicide. My suicidal thoughts haunted me even more because of my religion and culture; I was always taught that committing suicide is a sin. So, I built up a wall to keep them away from me because their constant, judgmental words were hurtful.

I work, go to school, and have made cool new friends. I have a girlfriend, but I will not bring her home because I don't want my parents or family members to judge and reject her. I am working on being happy for myself. Soon I will be leaving home so I can heal emotionally and freely live with my new girlfriend. If my parents, siblings, or other family members wish to visit me, I will welcome them with open arms.

I KNOW WHO I AM

I was no different than other 15-year-olds
And like many teens, I happen to like only girls
I deserve to be respected for who I am
My homophobic parents wear blinders; demand to
    see me in skirts and curls.

I came out to my closest friends hoping they'd
    accept me
I came out to my brother and sister, who gently tried
    to "fix me."
I came out to my inebriated dad, but it doesn't count
Slurring, he promised my mother would deny her
    traditions to accept my female lovers.

I thought my closest friends were real
They disappeared when I needed them most—they
    let me go.
My siblings chose not to cross la Cultura line
Being gay means going against stubborn Latino
    traditions and beliefs—it's taboo!

They refuse to see my deep wounds filled with
    emotional pus, the pain in my heart
Like a stream of mud full of anger, agony, affliction,
    and anxiety; debris gush throughout my body.

My walls continue to rise to keep those that bring
me emotional stress away from me
They choose to turn the other cheek—follow their
old traditions while denying my pain.

Why use religion and la Cultura to shame me?
Mom/Dad, why strap me under your traditional
Latino spell?
I feel alone, confused, drowning in sadness, and so
misunderstood
I hope my darkness will transform to light, or I may
bid all farewell.

Why can't my parents, or at least my mother, show
me she cares?
Why can't my family show or fake that they care?
Why judge me—I KNOW WHO I AM!
It's a burden that I must, on my own, bear.

You think my needs are not real
I'm not invisible, yet you ignore me
Why judge me—I KNOW WHO I AM!
Unapologetically, my name is Sonia, your daughter,
your sister, and I identify as nonbinary.

My parents wish I could disappear knowing, but not
admitting, they have a gay daughter.
They fake and say, "I love you" as long as I admit I
like boys instead of girls!
At 20 years old, I'm ready to leave home, but getting

emotionally stronger takes time
I wish I had their blessing, or maybe not because,
after all—it's just a word.

Letting Out!

Haiku and Free Verse Poems inspired by Warrior's story:

20 and STRESSED out!
Parents are ill yet working hard
Paycheck to Paycheck.

This devastating economy has financially impacted my parents and many other seniors who are on a set budget. My financial hardship is a significant stressor because my parents depend on me to help them meet their financial needs. The stress of helping my parents financially is intensified by the fact that I have an older, Mr. Cheapo, penny-pincher, and tightwad brother!

I don't want to suffer like my parents, living paycheck to paycheck. I'm in my twenties, and my parents are in their late sixties. I think my dad turned 70 years old last year. He is way older than my mom. My parents are not 100 percent healthy; my mom has diabetes and arthritis, and my dad has Grade-3 prostate cancer. Yet, both go to work daily to make ends meet. My parents are proud people and never complain about what they don't have. I'm so proud of them for all they have accomplished, but I worry for them because they are older, have severe health issues, and have a mortgage hanging over their heads.

The higher cost of living is taking a significant chunk from my monthly paycheck. I currently help with groceries, utilities, and part of the rent. The gas bill alone has tripled! It's so shocking, and as cold as it has been, and going to be, in the winter, we have no choice but to use our home heater. They don't say this to me, but I know they worry about the day I tell them I can no longer help them financially because I've decided to move out.

I am not a selfish daughter. I feel very guilty even thinking about going out on my own, but I must think of my future. My older brother moved out about five years ago and it was hard on my parents. After he moved out, he stopped giving my parents any money, and worse, he rarely visits them. I know they're hurt, but they don't say anything or tell him anything. When he does visit, it's like the "king" has arrived and they cater to him. It has always made me mad because the burden and stress fall on me alone, although I am not their only child!

When I was younger, my parents, like traditional Mexican parents, favored my brother, and when I complained, I was called "niña llorona mocosa." Now, I am my parents' "Angelita" (Angel). To this day, Mr. Cheapo, penny-pincher, and tightwad can still do no wrong! How backward thinking and offensive is that for us Latinx women?!

My parents don't only struggle financially; they don't know how to make appointments on the doctor portal websites and barely know how to use their cell phones. My parents depend a lot on me to accompany them to doctor visits, especially my dad because he speaks little English. I have to schedule their appointments around my work and school time, and that's very stressful for me! I also fear one or both dying (on my watch), not to mention my fear of them getting COVID-19 or (Respiratory Syncytial Virus) RSV.

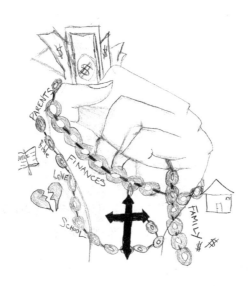

Letting Out!

I'm fed up with this outrageous inflation that is sucking
us all dry.
I'm seeing my parents (my viejitos) wilting away from
the stress of not making ends meet
I'm stressed because I, too, am financially tight—I'm
frustrated but can't even cry!

*I'm drowning, can't breathe, super-glued to
my Cultura!*

I'm a child of Latino parents.
I'm treated unfairly, and they never will care
I am many Latinx daughters who become family
servants!

*I'm drowning, can't breathe, super-glued to
my Cultura!*

I'm in my 20's and super stressed out.
I'm shackled with gender inequality of cultural injustice
restraints
I'm a niña llorona mocosa with many years of not
being heard, yet I'll never stop speaking out!

*I'm drowning, can't breathe, super-glued to
my Cultura!*

I'm my parent's emotional and financial support.
I am thin, 105 pounds. My masculine cheapo brother
is broad-shouldered and 275 pounds
I'm appalled he has never lifted a finger around the
house—a long story short!

> *I'm drowning, can't breathe, super-glued to
> my Cultura!*

I'm a daughter of two senior parents who are ill and
financially strapped.
I'm stressed about helping them keep their home
and maintain them as healthy as possible
I'm worried my viejitos still work super hard, are ill-
impaired, and handicapped!

> *I'm drowning, can't breathe, super-glued to
> my Cultura!*

I'm a Latinx feminist, a warrior, a survivor, who stands
against our patriarchal culture.
I'm feisty about my crazy and unjust cultura when it
comes to gender amongst siblings
I'm now ready to verbally put Mr. Cheapo in his place
during his next visit with my viejos!

> *I'm drowning, can't breathe, super-glued to
> my Cultura!*

I'm working paycheck to paycheck, like my viejitos—
my heroes.

I'm teaching my parents to use their doctor portals,
    but they refuse
I'm stressed and feel guilty thinking about my life—
    I must maintain my dominant superego!

I'm drowning, can't breathe, super-glued to
my Cultura!

Economic inflation combined with my culture stresses
    the shit out of me.
My extended family and mom have sadly adapted
    to being inferior beings of our traditions
I'm fighting our cultural norms, riding out inflation,
    but let it be known I'm not a nobody—I am
    a warrior Latinx female!

Only I Can Purge My Burdens

Haiku and Free Verse Poems inspired by Cindy's story:

> *My heavy world sucks;*
> *Must purge my hectic burdens,*
> *Now I want control!!!*

Controlling my life's burdens is like surfing in the ocean. Sometimes the waves are calm, and most of the time, things get out of control faster than I can manage. I am the middle child of seven. My parents are both immigrants. Since the age of seven-years-old, una niña pequeña, I had to translate for my parents at stores and clinics, and when we had to go in to pay the electric or water bills. I also had to take care of my younger siblings because my older siblings flew the coop as soon as they could.

By high school, I was trusted and responsible for paying the house rent. I was also the one to read and respond to debt letters.

Your payment is late!

I'm sorry, it's coming.

My parents made me feel super special, like a powerful Aztec Warrior Princess, nurturing and controlling the world in my hands. I could do nothing wrong! My younger siblings would seek my advice about school and friends instead of going to my parents. I was the parent-ified child, catering to my parents and younger siblings' needs.

I still had to focus on completing my homework and maintaining good grades to show my parents that I had the strength to control everything, including doing well in school. I know my parents appreciate my consistent contribution to helping them and allowing them to be overly dependent on me. Unfortunately, nothing much has changed. It's hard to say "no" to my parents, whom I love very much!

I don't know why I feel so damn guilty when I can't always help. My other siblings can do their part to pitch in but always find chicken shit excuses or say they are "too busy." My siblings and I are now older, in our 20s–30s. Most of my siblings have children and

spouses. I am not married, although I do have a girlfriend (in secret). My parents are my closest family, although I try to be there for my nephews and nieces.

My world is heavy because I've allowed myself to be sucked into my parents' life of burdens. Somehow, their burdens have become mine. I think my parents have become passive and helpless because I've done everything for them. I've got to let those lingering, overbearing burdens go and cut the emotional ties with my parents. All I want is to just be their child like my other siblings. I've got to begin to say "no" or "sorry, I can't help you this time," and then not beat myself up, but I constantly hear my inner voice tell me what a terrible person I am to my parents. These inner thoughts make me feel shitty, ashamed, and disappointed!

I have my own 25-year-old life full of hectic burdens. They don't realize it, but I'm jealous of my siblings for pulling away from our home life and making their own. Now, I want to do it for me because I deserve it. What is so wrong with that? Most importantly, I want to come out and be openly gay without feeling rejected or shamed by others. I want to hold my girlfriend's hand when we go out. My wish is for my siblings to accept me for me. My heart will be so happy if my culturally traditional parents accept me!

I wonder if any of them would be brave enough to carry my burdens, as I've proudly taken care of their burdens all these years.

Only I Can Purge My Burdens

My FAMILIA
Cantos con amor y cariño—también the unreasonable
      arguments, críticas y regañadas
      Enmeshed and dysfunctional
Homemade comidas to stay healthy—but the younger
      unapologetic generation prefers fast foods
      Enmeshed and dysfunctional
Muchas fiestas, piñatas de lindos colores—también
      muchas borracheras, peleas e insultos
      Enmeshed and dysfunctional
Grande familia, casados, con muchos hijos—they harshly
      criticize each other, but I still love my family
      Enmeshed and dysfunctional

My BURDENS
Feeling like Atlas, enslaved in holding up the hectic,
      chaotic family burdens on my shoulders every day
      Purge my burdens now—without shame!
Feeling like Sisyphus, slowly rolling the immense
      heavy bolder uphill containing MY burdens

Purge my burdens now—without shame!
I am Chalchiuhtlicue, fuerte Aztec Goddess of water
and protector of women and children
*Feeling brave to come out to my family—the heaviest
burden I've been carrying for a long time!*
NOW taking control of my life—while purging
my inner critical voice of shame!

Fighting My Inner Demons!

Haiku and Free Verse Poems inspired by Ace's story:

> *My life is fucked up*
> *I don't belong—or do I;*
> *I'll deal with my shit!*

I know my life is fucked, but who cares? I am a loner and only feel good when I'm high. I don't give a shit what people think of me. I enjoy smoking weed. I use drugs; meth, crack, and fentanyl. I don't need you or anyone to feel sorry for me because I don't feel sorry for myself.

I am the youngest of five brothers. I don't get along with my older brothers except one of them, so, as far as I'm concerned, the other three don't exist. When I was in high school, my mother passed away from fuckin' cancer, and my alcoholic dad couldn't deal with it, so he split—took off. I was only fucking seventeen, and that alcoholic asshole abandoned me. If roles were reversed, my mom would have never left me.

I'm now twenty-five years old and sometimes I work,

but most of the time, my aunt (my mom's sister) supports my "bad habits" to keep me from stealing. She's like a second mom, a sweet and loving aunt who closely resembles my mom's looks and manners, especially when she tells me off. I live at her home because I can't afford to live on my own. I know she cares for me, but I can't do what she asks me to do. She wants me to go back to school to get my GED. She tries to guilt trip me, telling me that my mom would want me to finish school. The problem is, I don't give a shit about that stupid piece of paper! She wants me to work and stay drug-free. Sometimes, I try to stop using to make her happy, but I've got demons inside me that kick my ass when I try to get clean, so I don't stop.

Don't get me wrong, I want to change, but I can't, or I don't know how, or maybe I don't want to. I know I'm hurting my aunt and brother, who is two years older than me and who has a steady job. Both have tried to help me with "interventions" to stop using, and I do stop for a little while but then go right back to my old habits. They get pissed off at me, and I get pissed off at me too! It's all stupid, but then I get mad at them for trying to change me. So much crazy, stupid shit has happened in my life.

I have friends. We all hang out and use together. They tell me that I'm the life of the party, but that's bullshit because how would they know since we are all fucked up whenever we get together.

Last year, I overdosed on fentanyl, and my aunt found me unconscious on the kitchen floor and called 911. That lady saved my undeserving life because she fucking knew how to do CPR. I was released from the hospital after about six hours and sent home. I've never been to a treatment center, which my brother wants me to do as part of his "intervention" to help me stay clean. The way I see it is that, if the damn doctors from the hospital did not send me to a treatment center after knowing that I use heavy drugs, like fentanyl, and OD'd, why should I listen to my brother? He doesn't understand my world. I don't like to feel my emotions, so I deal with them through drugs and drinking.

A social worker at the hospital told me to see a therapist (she even gave me a list of therapists to call) because she told me I had "important losses"

in my life that I had never dealt with. Damn, I'll deal with *that* shit on my own time. I hate to see my aunt crying, praying for me, and begging me to stop using. She tells me I am different when I use drugs or drink. I tell her, "Tia, when I'm ready, I know I can stop." I know she cares.

A couple of my friends, who also have OD'd, did not make it. They died, and that's pretty fucked up! I think about them a lot. Then I think about my aunt and brother who truly care for me.

Fighting My Inner Demons!

Drinking, drugs, and partying is dope
I feel fucking free when I'm high.
Getting wasted and forgetting *me* is my escape
So fuck off, and let me glide down that so-called
      dangerous slope!

We all suffer family and friend losses
What's so different about my way of coping with
      that shit?
I'm angry, and I use; I'm lost, and I use; I'm happy,
      and I use; I'm pissed off, and I use
My inner demon voices have their fucking way of
      forcing me to carry my life crosses!

To OD and make it back was a fuckin' miracle
I'm told I'm a broken person with skeletons in my closet.
Using is my way of coping, relaxing, and fighting my
      demons away
I am getting tired of coming down from my highs
      and feeling fuckin' miserable!

      It's time to get clean—to fight my inner demons!

¡Eres Pendejo!

Haiku and Free Verse Poems inspired by David's story:

¡Eres Pendejo!
Abused childhood memories.
GROWN UP—and coping!

I grew up in an abusive home. There was no such thing as "feeling sick," or "My tummy aches," or "Mommy, Daddy, I hurt my leg." Nobody cared. I am one of four siblings, two boys and two girls. Our father tormented us and constantly beat us. He didn't see us as his children, he saw us as a disturbance.

My father would selfishly bring home warm food (a thick burrito packed with fresh beans, beef, and salsa) for himself and would eat it in front of us, knowing we had not eaten a complete meal in two days or longer. We were starving so much that sometimes our stomachs would rumble uncontrollably as we secretly watched him savor every bite. When he'd catch us looking at him hog up, he'd say, "No les traje comida porque están muy gordos." He'd also take forever using the one bathroom we all had to use in our small, one-bedroom house, and although we begged for him to allow us to use the restroom when we badly had to go, he yelled back, "Aguántense."

He would scar us with his belt buckle, electrical wire, and tree branches. It was always so painful, but we tried to hold back our tears because we were taught that tears showed weakness. He'd say crazy things like, "I won't stop hitting you because you keep crying." Sometimes when he beat us, we bled, and he would say stupid shit like, "Believe me, it hurts me more than it hurts you," or "Creénme, ésto me duele más a mi que a ustedes." What crazy thinking from this devil dad! Worse than him beating any of us kids, though, was watching him beat my mother.

"You all know she deserves it." He'd then repeat it in Spanish, "Ustedes saben que ella se lo merece."

My father is like Dr. Jekyll and Mr. Hyde; sweet one day, and evil the next moment. His unpredictable personality changes (whether drunk or not) drove us all crazy for years. I feel bad that we were too scared to defend my mom. If we tried to intervene, she'd tell us off for getting involved because, in her mind, it was better if he hurt her and not us. My mother was an abused woman who couldn't even defend herself, let alone protect us from this evil man we called Dad. We were not a normal family.

Growing up could not happen fast enough. As each

of us turned 18, we got jobs and moved out. I don't know which was worse, the physical pain he carved in our souls or his daily abusive, mortifying, humiliating, demeaning, insulting words. "Que dirá la gente de ustedes tan estúpidos, idiotas, pendejos," etc.

The evilest part about him was how good he was at tearing apart our dignity and respect for ourselves. He loved pitting us against each other, and then he'd tell us, "En la calle, vale más que se protegen uno al otro!" (In the streets, you better all protect each other). We were his punching bags, the boys as well as the girls, and my mother was a battered woman. My father's crazy, evil personality overshadowed the one or two days each month that he was actually nice to us.

Most of the time he was drunk, but again whether drunk or not, the physical and emotional abuse was constant. Sometimes, he would beat us and suddenly tell us to get in the car because he wanted to buy us all ice cream or donuts. To keep him briefly happy, we would go, smile, and thank him for the treats. We felt repulsive eating his treats as he'd forced us to smile and show him joy while eating them. We may have looked normal, but we were not a typical family. Both of my parents have passed away now, and I thought that if they were gone, I'd be free. I was wrong.

I am now 25 years old. The physical scars are simply grill markings on my body, as well as those on my siblings. Sadly, we had nothing else to do for fun but compare our body scars–who had more and where. My evil dad's voice of negative thoughts continues to plague me, as if my father is still here abusing me. His negative, abusive thoughts torment me every time an opportunity comes up when I have to make a reasonable adult choice for my well-being. That is my struggle!

¡Eres Pendejo!

Like many very young children, I loved and admired
　　my dad.
Then, the verbal, physical, and controlling abuse
　　started and lasted a lifetime.
Tension and ambivalence created mixed feelings
　　about my dad—Dr. Jekyll and Mr. Hyde.
He was also known as the Tasmanian Devil because
　　of his sudden mood changes.
　　He is dead, so why does *his voice* still haunt me?
¡Eres pendejo! ¿Qué pensará la gente porque eres
　　un inútil.? ¡No sirves para nada!
He'd scar us with his belt buckle, electrical wires, and
　　he also tore branches from a
beautiful lavender, hibiscus tree that stared into our
　　front window and witnessed his daily abuse.
Branches that were not meant to be used as weapons
　　on children's bodies.
　　He is dead, so why does *his voice* still haunt me?
Strangers who meet him say he speaks intelligently
　　and is respectful, friendly, and hard-working.
My dad is like Dr. Jekyll, caring and loving for a very
　　short minute; then
melodramatic, intense mood swings suddenly come

over him.

My dad is now Mr. Hyde, an exceedingly cruel and
violent man tormenting us for days!

He is dead, so why does *his voice* still haunt me?

No more rivers of tears dared cover my cheeks, piel
de canela.

I still hear his voice repeatedly putting me down—in
my head.

Me avergüenza que seas parte de esta familia.

Yet, we all strongly felt the same about him—ashamed
of our manipulating monster dad.

He is dead, so why does *his voice* still haunt me?

I grew up in an abusive home, watching my mom get
tortured by my dad's bare hands.

He pulled her hair, punched her face, and spit on her
while telling us she deserves these beatings.

As children, we were shocked, speechless, and too
scared to help her from Mr. Hyde!

We thought our monster dad would murder our
battered mother or one of us.

He is dead, so why does *his voice* still haunt me?

Therapy is for crazy people—so I thought.

That is what his voice told me for many years until I
realized he was wrong!

Therapy is for those who are emotionally hurt and
need a caring professional who listens.

I am working on getting rid of his negative devil voice
in my head.

He is dead, so why does *his voice* still haunt me?

He is a true charmer to others but a controlling, giant ogre to his wife and children.

While uttering his stupid, asinine words, *Creéme, ésto me duele más a mi que a ustedes.*

We all hated Dr. Jekyll's fake grin as he'd invited us to eat ice cream after the beatings!

His bizarre, two-faced behavior made us feel hyper-vigilant and crazy.

He is dead, so why does *his voice* still haunt me?

I work and eat when I want to—no more starving!

I use the restroom in my leisure time—no more holding it and later getting stomach aches!

I avoid fake, abusive people like my dad—Dr. Jekyll and Mr. Hyde personalities.

Sometimes I feel insecure, but it doesn't last long like it used to. As my dad's voice fades in my head—I am coping!

Accepting ME When It Doesn't Feel Normal to YOU!

Haiku and Free Verse Poems inspired by Phil's story.

He, His, She, Her, Theirs
Normal—Different to you!
Accept me or not.

My name is Phil, and my pronouns are he/him/his. I have known I was different since the age of eight. I used to be a girl. I even wore the pretty dresses and girly, matching pantsuits my parents bought me for special family occasions and for our weekly Sunday mass. I did not come out to my parents until I was eighteen. Many kids who feel different at a very young age don't know how to explain to their parents what, or how, we feel. When we experience gender dysphoria and gender transitions, we need our parents to help us be okay and feel comfortable expressing ourselves. We also want our parents to try to understand, even if the gender change in their daughter or son confuses them.

I am twenty-two, and my parents still struggle with me being trans. I heard my dad tell one of my aunts, "I'm trying to understand *him*, but I keep fucking up because I have a hard time wrapping my head around my daughter becoming male." I moved out at eighteen because I saw how uncomfortable my parents were when they noticed the hair growing on my face because of testosterone shots. My dad would tell me, "It's just a phase. You'll always be my special tomboy. You'll grow out of it."

My mom would try to use the Bible to try to change my mind, "Please read the Bible and see if you can find peace and understanding for yourself." I know she was afraid that by me transitioning I would abandon God, which I never did, but that was her fear. My parents don't have to "get it" or understand it, because I know it must be difficult for them to see me trans from female to male right before their eyes. I merely ask that they try to accept me for me.

Growing up, I loved hanging out with guys *and* girls and had a steady group of friends throughout my school years. I maintained the gender traditions of going out with boys, although deep inside, I was beginning to like girls, and then later, I liked guys again. So, during my teen years, I experimented. I thought that maybe I was gay, bisexual, or pansexual, and not everything has to do with sex. Gender identity is about how you feel about yourself. For a while, I swung between genders; I was gender fluid, but now I know who I am—I'm Phil and I'm transgender.

Many parents might experience some grief or mourn when their child transitions, like me. In supporting my decision, I merely ask that they try to accept me for me, including my appearance, clothing, mannerisms, etc.

Society or close-minded family members may see me as oppositional, sinful, and repugnant. I've come to terms with knowing that people feel how they want to feel. However, I will not allow society or anyone to control my life. I don't need to accept their misunderstandings and judgments. I am not resisting societal norms or gender constructs. As a trans, I am describing myself as being true to who I am!

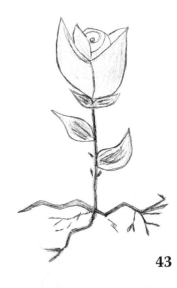

Accepting ME When It Doesn't Feel Normal to YOU!

Feeling abnormal is normal for me
Feeling misunderstood by my parents is normal for me
Feeling judged by family is expected, but it still hurts
Feeling judged by so-called friends is fucked
Feeling judged by others outside my circle is
     ignorance and bias
Look at your shortcomings before judging me!

Feeling inadequate because I'm trans...
     NEVER
Feeling guilty because I'm trans...
     NEVER
Feeling I failed because I'm trans...
     NEVER
Feeling I failed my parents because I'm trans...
     NEVER
Feeling I failed my family because I'm trans...
     NEVER
Feeling deficient because I'm trans...
     NEVER
Feeling like I'm "not a real man," because I'm trans-

male... NEVER

Feeling I'm weak and insecure because I'm trans...
NEVER

Feeling defective because I'm gay, bi, or trans...
NEVER

Feeling imperfect because I am in a female body...
NEVER

Feeling inferior different because I'm trans...
NEVER

Dealing with Bullies

Haiku and Free Verse Poems inspired by EM's story:

> *SOCIAL MEDIA!*
> *Classmates pierce my soul with hate*
> *Don't know YOU, so STOP!*

Getting through high school and college is hard enough without the added stressors of being bullied. It's so sad to see students bully other students for no reason. My experience being bullied in high school is a bit different than what I witness now in college, but there are bullies in both environments.

I see bullies roam the hallways and lunch areas in groups (never alone), looking for shorter and fragile-looking students to pounce on. The odds are better for the bully when they pick on a thin, heavy-set, or shorter student. Bullies come from all ethnicities and never fight alone with someone their own size or bigger.

What is most bothersome to me is seeing Latinx students putting down other Latinx students. So often in high school, I witnessed bully Mexican students punk other Mexican students. They start with, "You stupid, pendeja (asshole) Mexican. If you *are* Mexican, why can't you speak Spanish?"

These bullies get thrills when they punk other innocent students because of how they speak, how they look, where they shop, what city they live in, the color of their skin (which is a *big* one), how they dress, and so much more. Sometimes all it takes is you *looking* in the direction of oncoming bullies (in the school hallway) for them to punk you!

All the bullies want to do is to humiliate, intimidate, and shame other kids through fake social media. One insidious thing they do is create fake social media accounts about someone they don't like, and many students follow them! You want to make sure it's not you that they are after! I've watched bullies approach innocent students in the hallway and lunch areas. I've even seen them have the gall to walk into a class in session and disrupt it merely to shame someone publicly. All the students connected to certain social media accounts get a notice of which student the bully will punk next. Before you know it, the actual argument and fight are on social media for everyone to see. Most teachers stop these fights, but some are afraid to get involved and call for help at the front office—for the innocent student getting beat up, that seems forever before help arrives.

I don't consider name-calling bullying, but that's how bullies usually start. Gradually, they continue to intimidate a person by staring at them, purposely bumping into them, then making up fake social media accounts to post videos of their victims getting beat up. I am connected to the fake social media accounts because it helps me to make sure that my younger sister will not be their next victim. In high school, I tried hanging out with her as much as possible. It was my way of looking out for her to protect her from these bullies!

Bullies are so ignorant. Skin pigmentation has nothing to do with a person's ethnicity! I'm biracial and always get called out for being "White" when I am not. I wonder who taught these people to be so racist and to intimidate others merely to humiliate them. Bullies are very insecure people! As a young person of color, I have enough stressors to deal with in my life, and I hate that many of us also have to deal with bullies!

Dealing with Bullies

I see it and hear it almost every day,
"You stupid, pendeja (asshole) Mexican.
If you *are* Mexican, why can't you speak Spanish?"
SAD... a Mexican disgracing another Mexican.

Skin color means nothing.
Stereotyping spreads like a wild fire—IT'S A TRAP!
Flaming one mind onto another with no end in sight.
If you disagree with a bully, you WILL eat crap!

I've been told, "Your skin is fair, you MUST be White."
WHAT IS THAT SO SUPPOSED TO MEAN? No
        sensitivity!
I'm biracial. Latinx high school and college peers only
        see my light skin color.
My skin pigmentation has nothing to do with my
        ethnicity!

You're Dark Brown—you MUST be a wetback.
You're White—you MUST be money rich.
You go to swap meets—you MUST be dirt poor.
You shop at Kohl's or Target—You MUST be a
        higher-class bitch.

Bullies use fake social media accounts to intimidate

others.

"Tell me to my face the shit you said about me on
social media." Idiot, it's FAKE NEWS!

They bully for power, to gain territory, become
infamously popular.

The victim braces for the fight of their life—the
humiliating physical abuse!

Bullies run in packs and are never alone.

They surround and swarm whoever they perceive
to be fragile:

a shorter-statured victim for play.

Like sharks preparing for a feast,

their nails resemble shark teeth as they enjoy marking
their prey!

Pulling chunks of my hair, kicking me until I bleed or
break a bone,

threatening to kill me with piercing demon eyes—
I'm screaming.

I'm trapped, and the fear for my safety
is real!

I feel sharp objects penetrate my skin—Oh shit!
I'm bleeding!

Intimidating, judging, making threats, and superior
thinking are signs of a bully!

I wonder what their parents or family members
are like.

Bullies and those without a conscious don't think

before they speak.

Careful not to stare at a bully unless you are ready to be punked—to fight!

Fitting In When I Can't

Haiku and Free Verse Poems inspired by D's story:

> *I want to fit in.*
> *Youth to Adult... It's fucked up!*
> *Always felt awkward.*

Growing up was not easy for me. I wanted badly to belong, so I became a party animal and joined a gang to show what a badass I was. I did not want anyone to fuck with me. Although I was in a gang, I still felt awkward and lost in life. The truth is that I was trying to fit in, and for some reason, I just couldn't.

My mom rejected me since I was a kid, maybe because she did not know how to show that she loved me. My dad was okay and there for me, but I wanted my mom to say the words, "Mija, I love you." Sadly, I don't remember that ever happening.

After high school, I got a clerk job at a company in downtown Los Angeles. Trying to assimilate into adulthood was fucked up because almost every adult at work was stuck up, so I couldn't relate. I was the youngest worker there. The adjustment was hard for me because, although I was 18, I did not see myself as an adult. I still drove my low-rider to work, and on weekends I hung out with my crazy friends (most did not have jobs) just to get high. What kind of life was that?

It's so awkward to not fit in while in high school, and then to not fit in as an adult. I got pregnant at 20 years old, and once I had real responsibility, my life took another turn. I did not marry the father because he was an immature asshole. I stopped hanging out with my homies because I did not want to expose my baby to that lifestyle.

I know my mom loves my baby, but she still can't show me love. I hoped my mom would change and show me a kinder and gentle heart, but nothing changed in her about me. I have always felt lonely and need more confidence to make or keep good friends.

It's been hard raising my son alone, but I will never let him down and always show him that he is loved.

I'm still young, so I'm not giving up on the idea of getting a house on my own and having a good husband who can show me love. If not, fuck it—I'll succeed on my own as a single mom. One thing, for sure, is that I have always shown my baby boy that his mama loves and cares for him. At 23-years-old, I now work in a healthcare facility and attend college to get my AA degree. I'm working toward getting my BS in Health. It's never too late to go back to school. My baby boy will be proud of his mom for never giving up!

Fitting in When I Can't

It's hard to fit in...
When the puzzle pieces don't match
When forcing a size seven foot into a size five shoe
When coercing your mother to love you—If not
By having a baby and sharing it with her.
It's hard to fit in...
When feeling lost in life
Wanting to be loved but afraid
Trying to find you is
Like looking for a needle in a haystack
When you have no real caring friends
But not confident enough to show your self-worth.
It's hard to fit in...
When I'm trying to get myself together
Unexpectedly, I became a mom too early, yet
Took on the responsibility of a loving mom
What is wrong with me that my mom doesn't accept
    me or love me?
It's hard to fit in...
ASSIMILATION—WHAT THE HELL DOES THAT
    MEAN to a person who her own mother
    can't even love?
I want to be accepted for who I am

I want to fit in—I will fit in!
I guess that begins with ME!

Why Shoot Us!

Haiku and Free Verse Poems inspired by SOS's story:

SHIT! Bullets flying!
Please do not cut my life short!
It's my LIFE to LIVE!

After the Uvalde Elementary School shooting, my outlook on school life has shifted to survival. I graduated high school and now I'm attending junior college. I walk around so damn paranoid, looking from side to side and constantly looking backward to ensure no one is following me. Before the recent school shootings and the damn shootings at the shopping centers, I have never felt so fearful, distrustful, and suspicious around groups of people. I'm sure many people think I'm on drugs because I look very paranoid whenever there are crowds of people around me.

I don't care what anyone thinks because I know how I feel. It's so messed up because I wasn't this anxious before all the shootings! I feel claustrophobic when I'm around groups of people, some wearing masks because of COVID and some not. Sometimes I have to get away from them because I get anxious and can't breathe. It's awful! My parents made me see a therapist because I stopped going to school for a while, although I love going to school, so I'm working on "getting back to normal"—whatever that means. In my classroom, I try to always sit far from the door and near a window just in case.

What is so confusing is that these peer-student shooters attended our schools. This means a dead student may have engaged with the shooter at their school sports, seen them hang out with their weird friends, and even joked around with them. These student shooters blend in with the rest of us trying to get an education. I don't understand why they would turn against us or go to an elementary school and murder children and teachers.

Twenty-one innocent children and teachers senselessly and sadly were murdered in May of 2022. Twenty-one family lives were destroyed that day. What the hell is wrong with people that think it is okay to murder? Crazy thoughts keep creeping into my mind of getting shot. I keep imagining my parents, my mom especially, freaking out. I also have awful thoughts of my parents or one of my siblings getting randomly murdered at the market, shopping center, church, or wherever there are crowds. I don't want my life destroyed by a mindless soul who loves killing people or has demons telling him to murder; I'm scared of that type of monster. If these shooters are so depressed, like many of us, why don't they talk with someone? Seek help. That's what I did. I have a therapist to speak with, not a damn automatic rifle. I think these shooters become hypnotized by watching and playing violent, bloody games. They love that shit and now use what they learned on their peers!

I can't stand the sight of blood, so thinking of blood splattering from other students onto me or my blood splattering everywhere is devastating and traumatizing. I haven't even lived, yet I have many crazy thoughts of dying at an early age. I'm so scared that I don't hang out before and after school, at school clubs, or with groups of friends. I've lost the feeling of safety I once had to hang out freely with my friends. Some of my friends told me to "get over it" and "go back to being the fun, party animal" I used to be. I wish it were that easy, but it's not. I'm too young to die, to be shot in cold blood… it's so messed up!

Why Shoot Us!

I HOPE I never cross paths with a peer-student
    school shooter!
Four shootings in colleges or high schools, all in
    California,
My home state... I don't want *that* to be the norm!
      Why Shoot Us!
      This is fucked up!
            Fighting to live,
            Yet I *haven't* yet!

Firearm bullets swarm these schools in the USA with
    flares of fire!
Students of all ages face fear every day from a
    possible peer-student shooter.
In a frantic fight to live or to die, bodies bathed in
    blood are splattered in the hallways and
    classrooms.
      Why Shoot Us!
      This is fucked up!
            Fighting to live,
            Yet I *haven't* yet!

A mindless, hurting student comes to my school
    armed and ready to cut my life short.

A sacred place of safety for years, making friends,
and teachers enticing our brains to progress.
We all become desensitized to people dying, maybe
from so much social media and violent video
games.

Why Shoot Us!
This is fucked up!

Fighting to live,
Yet I *haven't* yet!

You hunted down innocent grade school children in
Uvalde, Texas, in May 2022.
What did these innocent children and their teachers
do to you?
You cold-bloodedly shot them, saw them suffer, and
saw them take their last breath of life. Yet, you
feel like a victim in the end!

Why Shoot Us!
This is fucked up!

Fighting to live,
Yet I *haven't* yet!

Anxieties and fear crawl throughout my body. A
strong throbbing heartbeat–the panic button!
Every day I walk into my school where I used to feel
safe. I've seen you play in our school sports
games, and hang out with your friends. I didn't
know you carry a gun to school to hurt; so why
pull that trigger? And how dare you yell out,

61

"I'm the victim!"
Why Shoot Us!
This is fucked up!

Fighting to live,
Yet I *haven't* yet!

What angry demon drives you to murder? This act
does not make you a mighty hero,
A mean soul with no empathy for others who tortures
and kills small animals and kills people in cold
blood, yet you claim to be a victim!
We are real people, not a fake simulation like those
damn violent games you often play!
Why Shoot Us!
This is fucked up!

Fighting to live,
Yet I *haven't* yet!

Are you depressed, like many of us? Shooter, it's hard
to feel sorry for you!
PLEASE put your weapons down and hand over your
demon voices to a professional therapist
willing to help you get rid of your planned urges and
cravings of your violent actions.
But PLEASE don't pull that trigger!

What Does Size Have to Do with Anything?

Haiku and Free Verse Poems inspired by Will's story:

I am a big guy.
My feelings are important.
Racism is poison!

Since childhood, I've always been a big guy. I don't think my friends cared enough to know my birth name because I've been known as Tuba, Whale, Hippo, Two-Story House, Mount Everest, and so on! Out of cariño (affection), my family calls me "Gordo" (Fatso), and I'm okay with it. Outside of my family, they introduce me with my proper birth name.

I'm in college now, and I struggle to sit in those tiny classroom desks and chairs—they are too small for my size. People make fun of me, and some teachers have refused to let me sign up for their classes. I'm just a morbidly obese student who makes everyone uncomfortable. I struggle to get from one side of the college campus to another if I have to hurry to make it to my next classroom.

When I walk into the eating area, I feel the malicious, callous stares like sharp spears penetrating my soul. I hold tight to my family values—my "Willow Tree" legacy of strong, adaptable and loving family members. Like the willow tree, I am strong, flexible, and adapt to harsh and adverse environments. Even heavy people have the right to eat at any given time of the day. Heck, I too need my protein!

I am usually alone; some people are afraid of approaching me because of my size. I am no monster and will not hurt a bee. If you are a good person con corazón (with heart), you will value me for whom I am, as I value all people. Being socially shunned is hard, but I also understand that my health is important, so I signed up to see a nutritionist. I hope this time it will work for me!

My most significant stress is not being accepted as a productive citizen in life, school, and work. Big people have feelings and a good heart and want to be accepted by society, just like everyone else, regardless of color, size, ethnicity, religion, etc. Too much racism has divided us, and judging me for my weight is part of racism. Too many kids have committed suicide due to being bullied for being obese or different.

I hope my story will help be an eye-opener to those who criticize obese humans before throwing stones of hatred or judgment at others. I hope my story will encourage obese people to reach out when they are ready to make physical health changes.

What Does Size Have to Do with Anything?

Nature and people are appealing and interesting

I come from a legacy of a strong, large family, like a
healthy Willow Tree

Whose roots spread out and caress one another with
warm and earnest feelings

The Sun and Mother Earth ensure that each leaf
and branch from the Willow Tree are well
nourished—como mi familia buena y sana

Our thoughts, sizes, and emotional feelings swing
in rhythm to the wind's unselfish, different
directions

Like the Willow Tree, some leaves must separate and
go on their own

So, as I make my way through life, it feels different,
yet I hold on to my strong family values—
my roots

To confront the looks (not from the Sky) and whispers
(not from the Wind) but from people's ugliness
of racism

When looking at me, they say:

It's easy to lose weight; eat less and exercise. Stay
obese and die!

Damn, you are a massive whale—Moby Dick!
Please do not sit on my chair or sofa
Why did you allow yourself to get so morbidly obese?
Don't fat shame me—I was raised with a heart of
gold, and I have a great personality
My gentle heart provides genuine support with
affection, like the willow tree provides an
abundance of
Shade with affection of a cool breeze from all its
delicate, gentle tiny leaves on a very hot,
sunny day
I've done nothing wrong or bad towards anyone to
deserve being criticized for my size
Stare at me all you want—It won't change my size
I am as kind as they come; make time to know me.
I will do the same for you!

I Quit!

Haiku and Free Verse Poems inspired by Job's story:

> *COVID is so real*
> *The UGLY in people spiked*
> *There is no RESPECT!*

I am stressed because, since the pandemic, it has been hard to make ongoing appointments with a therapist or even find permanent mental healthcare. I am trying to take care of my mental health, and I use the mental health tools I learned when I did see a therapist, but they don't always work for me at the moment that I am being yelled at or harassed by customers.

I used to love my job, but since the pandemic, I hate it and hate going to work. I'm a store manager, and sometimes, people say rude things or demand that I "speak English." The problem is that I *do* speak English! Damn it, I was born here in the United States, and my English is perfect.

We also have the worst generation gap behavior ever! Many Baby Boomers are so racist, verbally abusive, and try to bully the young workers. I'm so sick of it.

Many individuals, again especially the Boomers, (in my work experience) were freaked out because our store ran out of much-needed items like hand sanitizers, toilet paper, and cleaning products when the pandemic hit back in March of 2020. It's been non-stop, even today!

That's why I have Covid-Post Traumatic Stress Disorder (PTSD). Many days, I have experienced customers getting upset and yelling or swearing at me because they can't find a requested item in our store. What is wrong with customers who take their anger out on us workers? This continued Covid crisis and shortage of store items is not our fault. We have trouble keeping up with the demand.

Once, a customer loudly called out to one of the workers, "Hey, boy." This person is a nonbinary female with short hair. They are very respectful, and unfortunately, they feel discrimination almost daily. They did not engage. I stepped in and told the customer, "Please respect my worker." I was ignored. The customer continued, "We know you are hiding these items in the back for you and your workers." We walked away from that conflict.

I always tell my co-workers to walk away from

ignorant, prejudiced customers and report them to the upper management supervisors.

Every day that I force myself to go to work, I remind myself and my co-workers that it is not our fault for not having sufficient items on the shelves. I am losing faith in humanity. I've had older adults verbally poke fun at me in the store because I still wear my mask to work. These small-minded bigots take out their frustrations on us workers. It seems like these racist customers continue to use the pandemic as senseless, unintelligent, and ridiculous excuses to lash out when they can't find their essential items. They boldly push the limits of racism, discrimination, xenophobia, and intolerance if you are not of *their* race and generation group. Nowadays, they do not hold back and speak their biased, bigoted minds instead of being compassionate, respectful, and empathic humans. I don't need this type of work stress, so I quit! I am intelligent and will find a better job where I am respected. I am done with customer service jobs!

I Quit!

COVID! It is still E – V – E – R – Y – W – H – E – R – E,
      a horrible Pandemic once again
The virus, hospitals, needing oxygen, deaths, coffins—
      whispering *Rest in Peace*

Working in customer service has turned me into a
      frantic, unhinged employee

Rude, racist words submerge in and out of my pores—
      like red ants crawling, tearing at my skin!

The pandemic has brought out the ugly in people—
      raging, prejudiced customers!

I don't like living in this angry era. Verbal and physical
      violence has to stop!

My teeth bang loudly behind my mask, and every
      morning, my feet stop in protest of entering
      work to clock in

Customers scare the shit out of me—I can't breathe!
      I cringe to hear their nagging, fuming, biased
      voices

Their intense eyes cut through my mask, then blatantly
      disrespect me because of the color of my skin.

I still say, "Hello. Can I help you?" Since the pandemic,
　　　overt macroaggressions have flown off
　　　our shelves
Just to hear, "Speak in English damn it! Where's
　　　your supervisor, you worthless Latino liars!"

Just to hear, "Why are you wearing a mask? You think
　　　I'm going to infect you? How stupid are you!"

Just to hear, "Don't dare hide the toilet paper,
　　　bottled waters, the sanitizers!"

I'm in a panic, looking for a therapist to help me cope
　　　with these racist people!

They seem to have all disappeared—WHY CAN'T I
　　　FIND ONE?

When I show up to work, I am overwhelmed with
　　　COVID-PTSD!

Baby Boomer customers are the main bullies blaming
　　　us for store shortages; so foolish of them!
Waves of harsh and ruthless Boomer voices penetrate
　　　the petrified souls of young Millennials!
Unrecognized for working hard to stock all items on
　　　the store shelf as fast as we can at $12 an hour.

Don't hide the toilet paper, bottled water, the
　　　sanitizers—ready to maul us!

Who the hell do you think you are? Those items

belong to us—I ignore them to avoid being devoured.

Take that mask off to answer my questions!

What are you, Indian, Mexican, Armenian, WHAT?!

If you don't want to assist me because you can't understand English, get your manager!

I QUIT!
I don't need to be around ruthless, prejudiced customers—I will look for a job that pays more and honors respect at the worksite!

Calmness Beats Stress

Haiku and Free Verse Poems inspired by Robert's story:

> *My past... the Present*
> *STRESSING keeps ME from CALMNESS;*
> *Day-to-day trials.*

I stress out about everything. I'm told I am too skinny for a guy my age and height. I'm learning about nutrition and health in one of my classes. I get constant stomach pains and major headaches at different times at work, school, and home. I think it's from stress. It's funny, but when I'm gassy, the smell is so bad that I have to run out of the room before I become asphyxiated.

I just turned 23 and I live with a stepfather who has never cared for me. This was very stressful, especially when I was growing up, but I'm learning to live with it. I don't know my real dad. As a young adult, not speaking with my stepdad does not faze me because I don't need him. As a young kid, I sometimes felt disconnected from my family, including from my older half-sister and two younger brothers. Now, I can truthfully say that *they are* my siblings.

Many times, I felt trapped at home. I felt like I was living in a tangled web or a jungle with no way out. That was a significant part of my stressors growing up. I had many uncertainties about my present and future life. I am grateful to my girlfriend, Valerie, who has always been there for me. She is super calm, which helps me not get so worked up. I don't stress out as much when we are together.

I still live at home, and my relationship with my mom is pretty good. She gets it when I get pissed off, especially at *that man*! I can speak with her about anything. I work part-time, pay rent at home to my mom, pay my car insurance, go to a community college, and hang out with my girlfriend. That's enough for me!

I struggle with self-doubt and self-confidence. Sometimes negative thoughts come into my head, stressing me out because I struggle to concentrate. For example, I could be doing a worthless, irrelevant task, like fixing up my room, and a bad childhood memory creeps up. Those kinds of feelings ruin my entire day. I can't concentrate after that, and it pisses me off when I'm told I'm too defensive. I hate that I stress out for nothing because then I don't have the energy to eat, sleep, or do anything! You should see how many times I've taken the same class over and over.

I'm not suicidal, I'm saving money to pay for a therapist because I know I need one, but that will take some time. I have to pay out-of-pocket because I currently have a part-time job. I also need a nutritionist, but I can't afford one, so I did the next best thing and took a nutrition/health class in college. I'm learning so much from my teacher. I can ask him personal nutrition questions without being judged. This class has taught me that my stressors have messed up my gut. This is one class I will not drop!

My community college health center sees students as a number. They just refer me to career counselors. To see a therapist via platforms like Talk Space, I have to pay about $400 a month. I'm a survivor and will figure it out for myself. I wish young people had good, professional nutritionists and therapists readily available without going through so much red tape or paying so much money. Anxiety, depression, and stress are the highest concerns for my college-age group!

Calmness Beats Stress

I am stressed and live with self-doubt; I think I'm
  not depressed.
Negative self-talk runs downstream, yet no thoughts
  of suicide.
A college student working towards a successful future
  but can't ignore the past.
Stomach pains, headaches, etc., my twisted body is
  torched and harassed!

Stress... Stress... Stress!

Can't eat, can't sleep, and feel weak.
Strong, silky spider web stings hold down my life
  at home
like a lifeless puppet hanging from a piece of wood—
  can't even speak.
It's a lifeless, tangled cobweb—can I outgrow this trap?

Stress... Stress... Stress!

No denying how much I love my mom and siblings.
Growing pains of family shit build undesirable anxieties.
My emotions are hijacked.
Unaffordable mental health therapy—too costly to
  fight my inner enemies.

Stress... Stress... Stress!

I'm a survivor always looking for remedies.
Got to be resourceful to beat my STRESS.
Need a therapist and a nutritionist to feel healthier.
Now learning to breathe, eat healthier, and sleep! I
     know CALMNESS will keep me from darkness.

Don't Let Stress Keep You From Success!

Resources

We all need compassionate support from professionals to help navigate life's stressors.

The following resources can guide you to connect with counseling centers, nutrition/wellness centers, and other community resources. Take a chance and reach out. You may gain new, fostered relationships which are critical in your efforts to address your stressors.

Counseling Centers and Websites

Latinx Therapy
latinxtherapy.com
Provides podcasts, workshops, wellness resources, mental health professionals, etc.

Joon
joon.com
Therapist referral site for teens and young adults.

TherapyTribe: a Wellness Community
support.therapytribe.com
Free online wellness support community.

State of CA–Health and Human Services Agency
chhs.ca.gov/youthresources
Youth-focused mental health resources listing.

Mental Health America
mhanational.org
Mental health resources, including information in Spanish.

Speaking of Hope
speakingofhope.org
This website was created to be the go-to site to connect young adults who have lived mental health experiences. The site was created by young adults, for young adults and includes resources, job boards, and support group listings.

ULifeline
ulifeline.org
ULifeline is an anonymous, confidential, online resource center where college students can be comfortable searching for the information they need and want regarding emotional health.

Go Ask Alice
goaskalice.columbia.edu
The Go Ask Alice! site is supported by a team of Columbia University health promotion specialists, health care providers, and other health professionals, along with a staff of information and research specialists and writers.

LGBTQ Center–Orange County
lgbtqcenteroc.org
Provides a variety of health services and resources for members of the LGBTQ community in Orange County.

Riverside Pride
riversideprideie.org
Provides a variety of programs and events supporting members of the LGBTQ community in Riverside County.

Covenant House
covenanthouse.org
Provides information and resources for unhoused youth, including the operation of shelters across the US.

Sandy Hook Promise
sandyhookpromise.org
Information and resources for understanding and preventing school gun violence in your community.

Real Deal on Fentanyl
realdealonfentanyl.com
Information and resources for preventing fentanyl use and reversing overdoses.

Crisis Hotlines

Los Angeles County Department of Mental Health– Mental Health Access Line
(800) 854-7771
Confidential, Bilingual; available 24 hours, 7 days a week

East Los Angeles Women's Center
(800) 585-6231
Confidential, Bilingual; available 24 hours, 7 days a week

Crisis Text Line
crisistextline.org
Text HOME to 741741 from anywhere in the United States, anytime. A live, trained Crisis Counselor receives the text and responds, all from their secure online platform. The volunteer Crisis Counselor will help you move from a hot moment to a cool moment.

National Suicide Prevention Lifeline
(800) 273-8255
Connect with a crisis center closest to your location; your confidential call will be answered by a trained crisis worker who will listen empathetically, work to ensure you feel safe, and help identify options and information about mental health services near you.

Disaster Distress Helpline
(800) 985-5990

The Substance Abuse and Mental Health Services Administration (SAMHSA) Disaster Distress Helpline provides crisis counseling and support to people experiencing emotional distress related to natural or human-caused disasters.

Addiction Helpline America
(844) 561-0606

addictionhelplineamerica.com

Confidential; available 24 hours, 7 days a week; provides resources for finding rehab centers and supporting loved ones who are seeking treatment

Nutrition Centers
Los Angeles County–Department of Public Social Services
dpss.lacounty.gov/en/food.html

A comprehensive listing of free or low-cost food and nutrition services in Los Angeles County and the State of California

Community Opportunities
DSTL Arts
DSTLArts.org

DSTL Arts is a nonprofit arts mentorship organization that inspires, teaches, and hires emerging artists from underserved communities. Learn more about our programs; the Poet/Artist Development Program; Art Block Zine; Aurtistic Zine; Conchas y Café Zine; and our Creative Impact Workshops and Books at DSTLArts.org.

Other
(write in your own successful resources):

Acknowledgments

I feel so lucky to have a professional and compassionate team of mentors supporting my efforts to complete my chapbook manuscript. Thank you, Angie, Abraham Jaramillo, and Luis Antonio Pichardo, Founder/Executive Director of DSTL Arts. Overall, DSTL Arts genuinely highlights how everyone works together—a familia con pasión to artistically continue learning and creating. Familia, I greatly appreciate your ongoing support and encouraging words to keep writing this chapbook for all to enjoy reading.

A shout-out and special acknowledgments go to Melissa Zuniga and Walter Steve Zuniga, both illustrators, who collaborated to devote their artistic talents to creating images inspired by the poems and stories from this chapbook manuscript.

I greatly appreciate Sarah McMahon–Editor. Thank you very much for agreeing to review my chapbook manuscript. I value and respect your opinion, which helped me to improve this manuscript.

Con cariño y amor, I am blessed and thankful to all my family members and appreciate those who were able to make time to review and provide me with valued "honest" feedback about the poems from this chapbook. I know I can always count on you to support my efforts to accomplish my goal of getting this chapbook published. I LOVE you forever, your Sister and Auntie "Titi" Rose.

To my dear friends, thank you for being such special people who continuously support and inspire my creative efforts to grow, achieve, and teach through the arts. I appreciate and respect that you took the time to review this chapbook manuscript and provide me with your constructive comments.

–Dr. Rosie

About the Author

Born and raised in East Los Angeles, Dr. Rosie Ramos, Ed.D., MSW, worked as a bilingual social worker for 30+ years with predominately Latinx families in Los Angeles, Riverside, and Orange Counties addressing the daily stressors and family matters that young people, as you, experience daily. She also worked in the field of Early Education for over 20 years.

Dr. Rosie experienced family and social pressures growing up, like the one-sided, traditional Latino hierarchy and unjust double standards between male and female siblings. She experienced mistreatment and discrimination at the age of 10-years-old (for two years) from her same elementary school teacher, and again re-experienced the education inadequacies that teens still face today. She was involved in the 1968 East Los Angeles Walkouts, a civil rights march to gain access to bilingual education for all Latino youth.

As an artist, Dr. Rosie wrote educational plays (1980's through 2002) addressing the war on drugs, domestic violence, date rape, anti-smoking, HIV/AIDS, etc. She also hired youth from all ethnicities and community gente to perform her plays (teatro style) to impart social awareness affecting Latinx families, youth, and children.

Dr. Rosie is a published author of *Teach Me with Cariño: Head Start Teachers' Perspectives of Culturally Responsive Pedagogy in Preschool Classrooms* (2018). She later self-published *Compassion is NOT Weakness!* (2019) and *The Journal-Compassion is Not Weakness!* (2020). She engaged in several writing workshops and published an essay, *A la Fregada con el Chronic STRESS!!! (...regardless of what generation you were born in)* (2022) through the online publication *Saint Lunita Magazine* created by Las Doctoras: https://saintlunita.com/.

Poetry is a new artistic journey for Dr. Rosie. In January 2023, her first five published poems appeared in the *Conchas y Café Zine; Vol. VIII, Issue 1: See My Words*, a DSTL Arts publication.

DSTL
arts

This publication was produced by DSTL Arts.

DSTL Arts is a nonprofit arts mentorship organization that inspires, teaches, and hires emerging artists from underserved communities.

To learn more about DSTL Arts, visit online at:
DSTLArts.org
@DSTLArts